So you think you're a BOOKWORM?

So you think you're a

BOOKWORM?

*Over 20 hilarious
profiles of book lovers—
from sci-fi fanatics to romance readers*

Jo Hoare

DOG 'n' BONE

Published in 2018 by Dog 'n' Bone Books
An imprint of Ryland Peters & Small Ltd

20–21 Jockey's Fields   341 E 116th St
London WC1R 4BW   New York, NY 10029

www.rylandpeters.com

10 9 8 7 6 5 4 3 2 1

A CIP catalog record for this book is
available from the Library of Congress
and the British Library.

ISBN: 978 1 911026 43 3

Printed in China

Designer: Eoghan O'Brien
Illustrator: Paul Parker

Contents

Introduction 6

THE BOOKWORMS

Introduction

The world is broadly divided into two types of people: the book lovers and the WHATTHEHELLDO YOUMEANYOUHAVEN'TREADABOOKSINCE SCHOOL people. Now let's ignore that second type, for they are barely deserving of our attention, and focus on the ones who matter.

Presumably you, dear reader, are a bookworm; otherwise it's very unlikely you'd bother to cast your eye over this Introduction. Unless, of course, Great Aunt Jean bought this book for you as a passive-aggressive Christmas gift and you're politely flicking through before sandwiching it on your shelf between your two football autobiographies and that one Dan Brown you had to read when you went away with that ex who you really should have called it off with before you got on the flight, but hey the tickets were paid for... We digress.

Back to those who matter, and the term "book lover" covers one hell of a broad church. From serial book clubbers to sci-fi addicts via erotica obsessives and crime-aholics, there are as many different types of bibliophile as there are pages in that Paul Auster you've nearly put your back out carrying around. And we've got a profile of them all.

As well as finding out exactly what kind of reader you are (FYI, there's no shame in any of them... well maybe just a touch of shame, but who's judging?), there are also quizzes to further determine your commitment to the written word. There's some handy advice on how to interact with other bookworms who might not share your exact preferred sub-genre—especially handy if you'd like to ask out a fanfiction writer or share the bedside "to be read" pile with a series binger.

So go forth; work out what you are. And then, if you need to, lie to all your friends. We won't tell anyone...

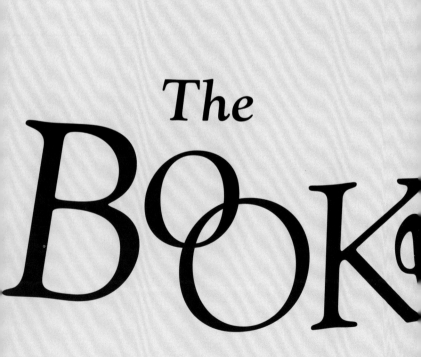

The

B❁❁K

The Binger

Not just confined to Netflix any more, if you've got a friend who is always "too busy" for social engagements, hasn't been "last online" for days, and has a huge collection of milk bottles on their doorstep (OK, that last one is a bit far-fetched; no one gets milk delivered any more, or in fact has dairy in their diet, and only millionaires have their own doorsteps), then he or she is probably a book binger.

Fighting hard against our collective diminishing attention spans, The Binger doesn't just manage to focus for the length of one novel, but for a whole series. That's a pretty massive achievement at a time when having to sit through a commercial break feels like an infringement of our human rights. Of course, with the highs must come the lows. Starting an eight-book series is like an amazing first date—there's so much to come and you can't really ever see it ending. The last page of book eight feels very much like walking in on your partner in bed with the yoga teacher—you're bereft, despondent, and can't imagine you'll ever find another commitment like it. But then a friend recommends a new series, maybe a genre you hadn't thought of before, and although at first resistant, you find yourself picking up book one on a lonely night. Within 50 pages—BANG!—you're in deep and with five huge tomes to go, you can see this one sticking around for a while.

All this sounds rather lovely to be honest, so if you've never tried the book binge here are some series to think about.

FOR THOSE THAT HAVE BEEN HIDING UNDER A ROCK

Harry Potter by J K Rowling

An obvious one, yes, but if you're one of the four people in the world never to have given *Harry Potter* a go, this is a good place to start your first binge. Serious fans also commit to a binge re-read once a year.

FOR THOSE WHO NEED TO BE GRIPPED INSTANTLY

The Brigid Quinn Series by Becky Masterman

The story of an ex-FBI agent tracking down a notorious killer who murdered her colleague, this four-part crime series couldn't be more unputdownable if you covered it in glue.

FOR FANTASY FANS

The Dresden Files by Jim Butcher

With a whopping 16 books in the series, this is a long-term commitment, but if vampires, demons, and magic float your boat then you'll sail away with *The Dresden Files*.

FOR POTTER FANS WHO'VE FINISHED THE ANNUAL BINGE RE-READ

Percy Jackson and the Olympians by Rick Riordan

Who knew Greek mythology could be funny? Heroes, love, adventure, and characters you can't stop thinking about.

FOR NOSTALGIC TYPES

The Chronicles of Narnia by C S Lewis

Before Netflix, before box sets, and even before DVDs there was this series. What self-respecting bookworm didn't have the complete Narnia set on display in their bedroom as a 10-year-old, with Aslan's majestic face looking up at you from your cabin-bed bookshelf? It might be time to say hello again.

The Hogwarts Alumnus

Consider the following sentence if you will: "***Harry Potter***? Isn't that for kids?" Now, if you feel either a) ambivalent; b) in partial agreement; or c) "Yeah, it is isn't it?" then you have already ruled yourself out of this sub-category of book lover. However, if you find your blood pressure has risen, your fists have started to clench (makes holding the book difficult doesn't it Potter-ites?), and a 45-minute takedown of that statement has already formed in your right-side brain (yep, we went for the FANTASY side of the brain, because even you have to admit HE'S NOT REAL), then you should keep reading.

The *Harry Potter* series is less a set of novels (and a merch takeover of everything from butterbeer massage oil to a Ministry of Magic toilet seat) and more a way of life, but how much of a Potterhead (we know that's a divisive name, but what you gonna do, cast a spell on us?) are you?

Whenever you see a *Harry Potter* movie you wear...

A) Whatever I had on that day. I might make sure to take a sweater, movie theaters can get pretty cold.

B) Full cosplay, as an obscure character mind you—every faker will be turning up with a lame scar and striped scarf. Madam Rosmerta will fool the fair-weather fans.

What is Dumbledore's full name?

A) You mean that British actor who plays him? Michael something?

B) How dare you be so informal! It's Professor Dumbledore at the very least; his full name is Albus Percival Wulfric Brian Dumbledore.

When a new book was released you...

A) Had it on Amazon pre-order and then put it to the top of your "to be read" pile.

B) Camped outside a bookstore 12 hours before release day, then went to a midnight reading party in full costume and stayed awake until you'd finished it. Twice.

The word "always" makes you...

A) Think of sanitary towels.

B) Cry. Every. Single. Time.

We say "Patronus," you say...

A) "Never again. Tequila gives me the worst hangover."

B) "A form of advanced magic that Harry was the youngest wizard to master. Have you read Professor Lupin's writings on the subject?"

Ever written fanfiction?

A) No.

B) Yep, and sent it to J K 140 characters at a time via Twitter.

If you hear a *Harry Potter* quote you...

A) Only recognize it if it's got the words Hufflepuff or Slytherin in it.

B) Blurt out the book, chapter, and first-edition page reference in the manner of an evangelist preacher.

MOSTLY As

Never call yourself a fan in the presence of a true Pot-head. Who knows what they're capable of?*

MOSTLY Bs

You stopped reading after question one, so disgusted were you with the concept of Potter ignorance.

* Not much.

The Fanfic Obsessive

We say fanfic you say a) "Isn't that those people who write on the Internet about One Direction all being gay lovers? Or Sherlock and Watson being gay lovers? Hang on, isn't it all about gay lovers?" OR b) "The greatest hobby ever. I WILL NOT BE FANFICTION SHAMED!" No matter where you stand on this very divided genre, there's no denying fanfiction is getting increasingly popular. Sure, a lot of it is bordering on restraining-order levels of creepiness, and if you're erotica averse, fanfic is probably not going to be your bag, but as it gets more mainstream if you're in corner a) you're gonna have to learn a few things. Here's a crash course on what NOT to say to a fanfic fan.

- "Ooh, is your work like *Fifty Shades of Grey*? That was originally fanfiction wasn't it?"

- "Are you interested in proper writing too?"

- "If you're taking someone else's characters, aren't you breaking copyright law?"

- "Isn't it all written by creepy old men with no social skills?"

- "Or by teenage girls sharing their deepest fantasies with each other on boy band forums?"

- "Or repressed spinsters who reek of gin?"

- "Or people in prison who've not seen a member of the opposite sex for two years?"

- "What's the plot? Is the story all about you?"

- "Is anyone else I know in it?"

- "Am I in it? Can I be in it?"

- "Ha, I bet it's all about sex. What's the sex like?"

- "Yeah, it's probably like when I was into clean eating/planning/the ice bucket challenge. Don't worry, you'll get over it."

- "Well I guess that's a good choice of show/book/character to rework, because you'd struggle to produce something much worse than the original."

- "You're not seriously thinking you'll make any money from writing fanfic are you?"

- "Why do you bother, no one reads that stuff do they?"

- "Haven't you got anything better to do with your free time?"

- "Why not just write your own original fiction?"

- "Can I read it?" (When your sole intention is to laugh hysterically at their prose.)

- "Is there any chance it will ever be made into a real book?"

- "Are you lonely? Are you sure you just don't need to meet someone?"

- "Do you dress up in a costume when you write it?"

- "Don't you have any of your own ideas you could write about?"

- "Is fanfiction ever well written?"

- "Haven't you grown out of that yet?"

- "Don't authors hate it when people rip off their work?"

- "Isn't it super-popular among serial killers and shooters?"

The Clubber

Remember when you used to read books on your own? When the reason you liked novels so much was because reading them was a solitary experience and you didn't have to deal with the irritation of humankind to enjoy them? It was nice wasn't it? Until some people had to go and screw it all up.

Thanks to the birth of the celebrity book club—think Oprah/Richard and Judy (delete as per your side of the Atlantic)—reading now has to be sociable! You have to go to other people's houses! Get dressed! Talk to weird colleagues! Pretend you like white wine! Some people discovered they actually enjoyed an added communal dimension to their hobby. Not content with the odd bi-weekly casual meet up, these readers took socializing far more seriously, joining multiple clubs to sate a desire to tell a room full of acquaintances exactly what they thought about the disappointing subplot and story arc in the latest psych thriller.

A serious clubber plans a whole diary around book clubs. Madness! In case you don't believe us, here's the diary of one clubber:

MONDAY: THE FANCY ONE

Invite: Handwritten card with monogrammed envelope:

"October's literary soiree will be held 7pm sharp to 9pm at Vanessa's town house. A casual kitchen supper will be served."

Translation: "I go to Europe for my vacations and, as such, like to add a certain amount of *je ne sais quoi* to my social gatherings. The use of "sharp" dictates exactly the mood you'll get if you arrive a minute before 7pm, but turning up around 15 minutes later is OK— *Debrett's Guide to Etiquette* deems that fashionable after all. I've put a cut-off time so you don't get any funny ideas about staying later, I've got reformer Pilates at 5am. Oh, and in case you didn't pick up on it, 'town' house means I have a place in the country, too."

Book choice: Whatever *Vogue* recommended last month that won't take the au pair too long to read and prepare a few notes for. "Why have a dog and bark yourself, darling?"

WEDNESDAY: THE SERIOUS ONE

Invite: Google calendar. Recurring event. List of questions attached.

Translation: "Don't you DARE come back with a 'witty' 'reply all.' You either come or you don't. And woe betide those who come unprepared. If you haven't got a response to at least two-thirds of the pre-prepared questions (and they're not even the ones suggested in the back of the book or pinched off the Internet) you won't be asked back again."

Book choice: Something in translation so that the head of the book club can show off about having read the novel in its original language.

FRIDAY: THE BOOZY ONE

Invite: A WhatsApp group message followed by a chain of 120 texts going back and forth.

Translation: "No one's actually read the book this week; not all of it anyway. The triple-figure message conversation is to ascertain that 'BYOB' refers to bottle rather than book, and on the day of the meeting at least two people will still be asking what the name of the book is."

Book choice: Um, unfortunately you don't remember.

11 People You Find in Every Book Club

It's approaching 7pm on a cold winter evening. You are with a work colleague who has collared you into attending your first book club meeting. "What else are you going to do on a Monday night?" she asks. You've already used up your best "sick partner/mother/brother/ hamster" excuses to avoid the past six invites to Friday night drinks, so you accept and wonder if a book club really will be the hotbed of creative thought you're imagining. It might be, but it's more likely you'll find the following characters:

1. The One Who Never Reads the Book

Identifiable by the pristine spines of his novels and his hasty rewording of the back blurb (here's a hint: if he describes anything as a "*tour de force*," then he hasn't even opened it), the one who never reads the book doesn't set out to ignore the whole purpose of book club (ie reading the damn thing), it's just that he doesn't have any time. Ever. Sure he could read on the train/toilet/ in bed like the rest of us, but he's far too manic and important. And if you were so foolish as to ever question why he didn't read this week's book, you'll be treated to a rundown of his hectic schedule. His kids/office/dogs/yoga classes mean he's always busy, therefore an activity as relaxing and enjoyable as reading is only suitable for lazy and unimportant people like you.

2. The One Who Takes It Way Too Seriously

A color-coordinated filing system and a set of notes that'd take longer to read than the book itself, this person probably never realized her dream of studying English Lit at college, so now you have to suffer for her crushed aspirations. She never can just "like" something, there has to be a 20-minute lecture on an aspect of critical theory to justify even a passing opinion. Secretly you're a bit jealous. And you'll definitely be pinching a snippet or two of her critique to use at your rival book club.

3. The Two-timer

See number 2. She tests a few lines of argument at the trial-run meeting with her less-preferred side-chick book club. She then pinches all the good ideas that come up in that discussion to use at the A-game group.

4. The One Who Never Talks

You weren't quite sure he was even supposed to be there for the first couple of meetings. Maybe he was just a slightly confused houseguest who got a little caught up and then felt it would be rude to leave? By the fourth meeting you realized he was a fully fledged member, he just hadn't fancied talking yet. To anyone. About anything.

5. The One Who's There for the Booze

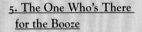

She opens her bag and out comes this week's book, swiftly followed by a bottle of red. Why? Because it's currently the only night her selfish husband comes home on time from work and, GODDAMIT, SHE'S NOT GIVING UP ON THE ONLY BIT OF "ME TIME" SHE HAS ALL FORTNIGHT. Book club is a legitimate cover-up for semi-drowning in Sauvignon that even her interfering mother-in-law can't complain about. The book-club boozer is the best person to sit next to if you found the book boring; she'll liven it up.

6. The One Who Just Watched the Movie

Giveaways include referring to the character by the actor's name and trying to pretend that by "soundtrack" he meant audiobook.

7. The One Who Clogs the Email Chain/WhatsApp Group

You all know the email chain/WhatsApp is only supposed to be for venue details and start times. Maybe the odd dietary requirement, because now Sandra's gluten-free you don't want her to get hangry. And as for the debacle when Mark the vegan realized there was an egg wash on those tarts, well no one wants a repeat of that. But there's always one who seemingly has nothing better to do all day than fill up your inbox with pointless crap. From "amusing" memes about books (we've all seen Grumpy Cat and the encyclopedia, LOL etc.) to hugely inappropriate personal details (yep, it is TMI that Geoff's prostate-related nighttime micturition means you're too tired to read today), you know every day will bring a new onslaught.

8. The One Who Doesn't Want to Talk About the Book

You're never sure whether it's just that he couldn't be bothered to read the book, he hated it, or he just would really, really rather talk about the Kardashians/Trump/the fact your host hasn't served the nice wine he brought and has instead fobbed everyone off with the cheap crap that you know is hidden in the kitchen. Whatever the reason, if this group member has his way the book's plot is but a minor inconvenience to a night spent gossiping.

9. The Host

This is the one responsible for setting the whole thing up; the person who gathered together this delicate mix of friends, colleagues, and an eccentric distant relative who is slightly easier to handle if she can be diluted in a group. It is the host who now presides over you all. She may use her power for good, but it may be for evil (for an indication of her intentions maybe ask who her favorite character is in the *A Song of Ice and Fire* series). Stay on her good side.

10. The One Who Always Disagrees

If you all loved this week's book, this member will have found it the biggest pile of trash since *Moon People* (FYI, read the reviews if you're not familiar). If you all loathed it, he's picketing the Booker prize judging panel until it gets a nomination. The one who always disagrees is there for the sole purpose of getting into a fight. Yes, he's incredibly annoying, but feel good about the fact that the time he spends with your group is probably the only thing holding his marriage together.

11. The Unreliable One

A creature of mystery, she never replies to the organizational WhatsApps and her appearance at the meetings is on a par with the northern lights in terms of predictability. You're not quite sure how she got involved with the club and neither is anyone else.

The Adulterer

Laying battered and discarded by the side of the bed, they were once shiny, new, and adored, but now their lover has moved on to better things. The seductive glint of that high-shine cover winking at them in the bookstore elbowed out the "3 for 2" pile of Scandi-noir chosen in an airport departure lounge. The once irresistible heroine of the turn-of-the-century romance pales into insignificance when compared to the half-human, half-radium-fueled-piston hybrid of a cult new sci-fi blockbuster. And as for that experimental novella on the parallels between second-hand cars and human suffering, well you can guess where that goes when the buxom Booker Prize winner walks into their life...

Welcome to the world of the literary adulterer, the type of reader who is unable to commit to one novel at a time. If books were dates this person would be ticking the box that said "in an open relationship." The Adulterer never sets out to cheat on a book, each new read starts afresh in the wake of another awkward crossover—"this book is the ONE," they think. And for a few glorious days it is. Never far from The Adulterer's side, this latest tome accompanies the bookworm on the bus, in bed, and at the breakfast table, pages crinkling in hot baths and cold rain.

The first third of the text is blissful, adulterers can't stop recommending it to everyone they meet and they've already walked into two lampposts and a medium-sized party of foreign-exchange students while trying to read it in the street. So far, so different... But then the doubts creep in. They hear whispers that there's something better out there, something new and exciting. They can't stop themselves sneaking glances at online book reviews before hastily deleting their history in case anyone should pry. The Sunday newspaper fiction charts call out, siren-like, to them from newsagent's shelves and they've invented an entirely new route to

work that means walking past the bookstore every day. Soon they're downloading free first chapters onto Kindles—it isn't really cheating if you don't buy the whole book, right? And if you don't meet up IRL, well, it's nothing. Of course, they can't stop there and before they know it there's a new addition to their literary harem. The dog-eared paperback that once was an inseparable companion is placed at the bottom of a very tall pile, only to be used months later as a coaster or doorstop.

The Adulterer can struggle to keep up with their multi-stranded ways. Despite best intentions, names are mistaken and forgotten (alas poor Yorick, I knew him, but there were others I knew better), plots become confused, and the probability of reaching the end is like pi: infinite. Is literary polygamy curable? There is one tried-and-tested form of therapy, so if you have an adulterer in your life or you suspect you're one yourself (admitting it is the first step), then this is worth a go: say hello to the WEEK-LONG HOLIDAY WITH ONLY CARRY-ON LUGGAGE. Forced to pack a maximum of three books (maybe four if you're off to a nudist beach), The Adulterer will be forced to read their way to the bitter end. Will it change them for life? Probably not.

The Book Thief

No, we're not talking about the Markus Zusak novel. Actually, we kind of are, because it's a pretty sure bet that any reputable book thief will have a copy or two of their namesake "borrowed" from pals that year EVERYONE was reading it.

That's The Book Thief's *modus operandi*, their pretend-temporary requisitioning nearly always focuses on the big sellers, the blockbusters, the word-of-mouth hits and "now-a-motion-picture" smashes. When a friend says, "You HAVE to read *A Girl on the Train/Fifty Shades/ The Da Vinci Code*," The Book Thief doesn't think, "Hmm, probably not, I read a page over someone's shoulder once and obsessive drunks/inner goddesses doing merengues/anything by Dan effing Brown isn't really for me." Instead, the ears prick up at this open invitation for a little light larceny.

Genre is irrelevant to The Book Thief; the only real motivation is a full bookcase and empty pockets—yours not theirs; you're the schmuck funding all this after all. If it's ripe for the taking, it's going in the BT's independent bookstore tote, which, come to think of it, was also yours. You got it for half price when you bought three novels that—hang on a minute—they've also still got! Next time you'll just put the money straight into their account.

Worried your collection is being depleted by a book thief? Read on to find the most common pilfering strategies. And if you "borrowed" this book from a friend? Well, they're probably onto you.

The "Slow" Reader

Mike knows he's got your latest John Grisham. You read it in three days on vacation and lent it to him for his weekend in the sun. That was 17 months ago and you've asked for it three times. You feel guilty every time, you've read it after all, but it's a fancy hardback and you've got all the others lined up together on a shelf. You also promised it to your sister, and why the hell are you making excuses? You're the one that paid for it in the first place. Mike claims he is STILL reading it. You have worked out that even if he read for one and a half minutes a day, skipping Sundays as a day of rest, he'd have finished the damn thing by now. Mike throws you titbits that he's nearing the end, mentioning the twists, the unveilings, the reconciliations, but as soon as you bring up the tender subject of the book returning to its rightful owner he's still got a few chapters to go.

The "Oh, I Lent It to Someone Else"-er

You can't quite decide if this person is just incredibly generous and giving (pretty easy with someone else's stuff, right?) or they're a total liar, hiding their ill-gotten gains every time you come round. Oh for the days of turning up at one another's homes without planning it three weeks in advance through a specific group WhatsApp chat, those were the times when you could catch out a fake lender.

The Out-and-out Denier

"You think you lent it to me? Oh no, I don't think so, I've never even seen that book. I've never seen any book. Ever. Definitely not me."

The Abuser

Are you the kind of person who takes great care of your books? The sort of bookworm who channels their inner museum curator and considers employing white glove protocol when handling your most precious novels? If so, then we suggest you turn the page now, for what we are about to tell you may haunt your dreams for the rest of your life. Say hello to the horror that is The Abuser.

This bookworm shows no desire to maintain the sharp angles of a creaseless page and cares not for the delicate spines of their novels. Instead, they place heavy bags on top of open books laid face down on hard surfaces, crushing spines like the marauding giant in the fantasy paperback they are reading. Rumor has it they've never even owned a bookmark! For goodness sake, surely everyone has an old receipt/train ticket/passive-aggressive note from a downstairs neighbor about leaving bikes in the hallway, within reaching distance that can be used to mark a page and save that poor novel's spine from cracking and creasing. But the abuser would overlook an avalanche of bookmark-able paper ephemera, preferring to leave their reads splayed and vulnerable.

The abuse intensifies on summer getaways, where pages left out in the merciless sun lose the hard-fought battle of glue vs heat and slip away across beaches and pools to meet a watery grave.

Speaking of water, the abuser is more than happy to read in the bath WITHOUT A HAND TOWEL IN REACH. They turn the pages with wet, soapy hands, caring not one jot that the paper will crinkle and shrivel. As for reading while carrying out other bathroom-related ablutions... Well, we don't even want to think about that.

The Abuser makes their books work hard for their money. At home novels double up as lap trays for dinners eaten in front of the TV. The latest chart topper becomes a doorstop, while the collection of Penguin Classics becomes a set of coasters for dirty coffee mugs. Others transform into spider squashers, computer-screen stands, tools to use to reach those ugly glasses in the top cupboard you only use when the people that bought them for you come round. If The Abuser ever manages to house these poor novels in the proper home of a bookshelf it'll be organized willy nilly, higgledy-piggledy; books squished and crushed with only dust and debris as bedfellows.

If The Abuser is out and about then things get even worse. Readers of a sensitive nature be warned, these monsters happily fold down the corners of pages to mark their place, worrying not what this mindless origami will look like once they reach the end. And if they need to note something down? Many's the work of fiction graffitied with phone numbers, appointment times, and shopping lists. Borrow from The Abuser at your peril, unless you have an interest in the date of their next colonoscopy or want to know if they're getting their five a day.

All of this isn't to say The Abuser doesn't love books, they really do. That's why they're so battered and beaten like a childhood teddy bear. Just don't ever lend them your copy.

The Cryer

Apart from in certain echelons of the BDSM community, it seems somewhat counter-intuitive that one's hobby should also render one hysterically tearful, but for The Cryer that's exactly what is demanded from a novel. If they haven't needed rehydration meds and a face wipe by chapter three, then they just ain't into it.

It's not any old sobbing The Cryer wants to do though. Sure there are books about unbelievable sadness, hardship, and cruelty that force even the most unsentimental reader on a busy commuter train to pretend they're suddenly yawning/have got something in their eye as the tear ducts fill up, but that's not quite The Cryer's bag. They're into crying as a genre and the WHOLE point of their favorite stories is to make them break down in floods of tears. (FYI booksellers, it wouldn't be a bad idea to start allocating a section of shelf space for blubbing and bawling; you could upsell Kleenex and waterproof mascara as "me toos.") For these readers, personal tragedy is king and it's not so much about reading tear-jerkers, but reading tear-climbing-in-your-eyes-and-frog-marching-that-saline-out-ers.

You might scorn The Cryer, weeping over a story that an unkind reader might consider to be ever-so-slightly schmaltzy, but actually they're onto something. A good sob over the story of a separated family or a little blub while reading about a never realized love affair is actually pretty good for us. Crying our eyes out relieves stress, promotes empathy, and, once the tears have been mopped up, leaves us feeling happier. Tempted to try? Here's a beginner's guide to sob-lit:

The Fault in Our Stars by John Green

Teens, love, cancer. A triumvirate of tears. This YA novel has caused many an adult to wipe snot with their sleeve when they've been caught without a tissue.

Any books by Jodi Picoult

Jodi is the queen of sob-lit. *My Sister's Keeper*—a story of a family torn apart when one sister decides she doesn't want to be a bone marrow donor for the other—is the most famous, but every single one is guaranteed to leave you a sniveling wreck.

The Lovely Bones by Alice Sebold

OK, we're getting a pattern here. Kids make us sob and this is no exception. Told from the point of view of a dead girl after her murder, make sure you're somewhere where no one can see you ugly cry.

Cold Mountain by Charles Frazier

There's nothing that can beat a big sweeping love story. Especially when it's a post-war tale of

heartbreak where neither party knows if the other is still alive. If you fail to cry at this, you should really consider whether you're human at all. Maybe it's time to get those circuits rewired...

Me Before You by Jojo Moyes

OK, the fact that Hollywood producers had the good sense to cast the not unphotogenic Sam Claflin in the starring role of the movie version gives this a teeny leg up on the weepie chart, but only the medically dehydrated could genuinely avoid the tears when reading this.

The One Who Definitely Judges a Book By its Cover

In the days before Instagram, The OWDJABBIC (yeah, not sure this acronym will catch on) wasn't into the written word—to him books were a bit old skool, and not in a cool vinyl record/vintage Hawaiian shirt kind of way. Sure, he still liked to read, but he was all about the Kindle. "A library in my back pocket!" he'd exclaim, fishing out an original non-backlight electronic reading device from his pair of original 1980s' 501s.

However, in the last few years something changed. The clever book industry realized that producing something considered "Insta-worthy" makes people between the ages of 18 and 40 66 percent* more likely to buy it. Hence the limited-edition artwork covers were born. If it's wrapped in William Morris, fashioned by fashion designers, covered in an individually numbered print of the *Yellow Pages*, or features a famous artist's reimagination of life in a post-technological world, then The OWDJABBIC would buy it.

Pinterest then helped pave the way with endless boards featuring dream libraries where books were arranged not in any kind of useful order— by author name or subject perhaps— but instead organized by where the color of a spine features on the rainbow. A well-stacked shelf kicking off with red all the way through orange, yellow, green, blue, indigo, and violet is a guaranteed triple-figure "likes" post and that's before you add hashtags.

ARE YOU AN OWDJABBIC?

Take this simple quiz to find out...

What do the letters TBR mean to you?

A) To be read.

B) To be recommended on Insta to people I don't know who are as unlikely to read them as I am.

* Statistics based on absolutely no evidence.

Your bedside table is...

A) Stacked high with books in various states of completion.

B) Made out of a pile of books with esthetically pleasing spines facing outward. Hardcovers offer just the right amount of surface area to support a letter-shaped neon light and a Diptyque candle.

Your bookcase is arranged in...

A) It's not arranged at all. You fit what you can in there with lots of books sat on top, higgledy-piggledy.

B) It depends on what your Instagram color theme is that month. At the moment it's monochrome, but you might change to jewel tones for Spring.

You buy a book because...

A) It's by your favorite author/ you read a positive review/ your friend really loved it.

B) It matches your nail varnish.

MOSTLY As
_____

Yeah, you like books because you like reading.

MOSTLY Bs
_____

Hmmm, yeah you might be a tiny bit interested in what's on the outside of a book, but hey, you do you.

12 Thoughts All Bookworms Have When They Go Into a Bookstore

If every time you step into a bookstore your bank balance takes more of a battering than the pages of your most treasured novel, then each of the following thoughts will be all too familiar.

1. The smell! I love the smell of books

Admittedly it's probably more the smell of the artisanal coffee and dairy-free cheesecake coming from the pop-up cafe on the 4th floor that hits you as soon as you walk in, but once you bury your nose in the first thick hardback you can get your face in... Then you know you're home.

2. Imagine I got trapped overnight!

FYI this has actually happened. An American tourist got stuck in a London branch of Waterstones bookstore a few years ago and the fool tweeted for help! That's like trying to make an escape from heaven.

3. How can I afford more?

What can I give up? Coffee, eating lunch, a kidney?

4. Why don't they have trollies?

For goodness sake, if they give me something on wheels to put in my one bag of prewashed salad and four avocados, then surely bookshops can help me out with my five hardbacks, seven paperbacks, and two new totes?

5. When will I read all these?

It's fine. I just won't sleep. Ever again.

6. Books are heavy!

Have they still not brought in trollies?

7. Is that the one?

OMG, imagine if I met my future love in a bookstore! We could have novel-themed invitations! A cake in the shape of our two favorite books! A wedding list at a bookshop! Oh no, they're reading *Fifty Shades of Grey/Jack Reacher*. Your dreams are shattered instantly.

8. Can I tell that person not to buy that book?

Will I look nosey? But it's so bad and you just know from looking at them that they'd far prefer to read one of my recommendations

9. Where do I start?

New in? Recommended? Maybe I should just do A–Z and check myself in for the next 72 hours.

10. How will I choose?

What do you mean I can't give them all a good home? But they all deserve my love? And splitting them up will be heartbreaking...

11. Right, I'm making a shortlist

OK, it's a longlist. A very long list.

12. I'll just sit down for a bit and read a few pages of each

When did it get dark outside?

The Reviewer

For The Reviewer there's no point in reading a book if you're not going to tell people about it. And whereas the majority of readers are happy enough passing on opinions about their latest read to friends/colleagues/to fill awkward silences while getting a bikini wax, the reviewer seeks a somewhat larger audience. They probably started with the odd few short reviews on Amazon (other bookselling sites featuring reviews are available, at least we think so... There must be, right?), then got high on the rush of power that came when two people found their review helpful. This was a mere gateway drug to the far more intoxicating Goodreads and from here it was the "bookternet" all the way. If you read a novel and don't tell people who you don't know about it on the Internet, did you read it at all? For The Reviewer the answer is very definitely no.

THE REVIEWER COMMANDMENTS

Thou Shalt Read the Book

Yeah, seems obvious doesn't it, but there's a helluva lot of one-star reviews out there saying things like "couldn't get this to download on my Kindle" or "bought it as a gift so haven't read." Hun, firstly, it's not the books fault you're a tech imbecile; secondly, a review isn't mandatory, no one is going to go to the house of the person you bought it for and reclaim it because you haven't bashed out 250 words on Amazon.

Thou Shalt Not Write Fake Reviews

Maybe your Goodreads is looking a little shallow... That beachside book binge has kind of messed up your status, but you didn't want to look like you hadn't been reading at all, so where's the harm in slipping in the odd Booker prize shortlist nominee? You've read the cover copy and a review online, plus you're definitely gonna read it at some point. That makes it fair game... Doesn't it?

Thou Shalt Rarely Give 5 Stars

No one will trust you if you say everything is brilliant. Add the odd 3-starrer and watch your stats go up.

Thou Shalt Stay Away From Drama

Rows with authors, calling out fakers, kicking off when your reviews are censored, let's play nice hey, guys...

Thou Shalt Not Fuss Over Numbers

Many's the reader weighed down by bookreading challenges. Who cares if everyone else on your reviewer social media is doing the book-a-week challenge. Think about it, does anyone actually check?

Thou Shalt Keep it Short and Sweet

No one needs a plot synopsis longer than the first chapter of the book, we can get that information by reading the blurb on the jacket. Just write something about your overall opinion of the story please.

How Much of a Book Lover Are You Really?

Fancy yourself as a literarian? Take this quiz to find out where you stack up on the bookshelf of life...

Have you ever seen a film adaptation BEFORE reading the book?

A) Of course, it's a good shortcut when I have no time to read the book.

B) Once or twice, but if it's my movie choice I wouldn't choose to.

C) Before or after makes no difference, when it comes to remakes it's a big NO WAY. I once accidentally walked past an open-air screening of *Emma* and had to keep my eyes shut for the next six hours as penance.

You keep your books...

A) On my bedside table.

B) I've got a few bookcases.

C) They keep me. Or keep me trapped in the house, because I've got so many novels that I can't actually beat a path to the front door.

On vacation you pack...

A) One book. I can swap it with my friend/partner/those weird crappy loan libraries of other people's Ambre-Solaired books that hotels always have nowadays.

B) Two books. And I'll probably buy a new one at the airport.

C) More books than underwear. I can't rinse a book in the hotel sink.

You'd read a book...

A) In bed, on a train, maybe in the bath.

B) At work (that Kindle phone app is a godsend for bathroom breaks), during dinner, at a boring party.

C) During sex, at a funeral, in a job interview.

What's the longest you can spend in a bookstore?

A) An hour if it has a good coffee shop.

B) A couple of hours max.

C) Longer than my last three relationships. Combined.

Your favorite book...

A) Changes all the time, I'm into Scandi-noir at the moment, because I enjoyed watching the TV shows.

B) Sits in pride of place on my bookshelf.

C) Changed my life. Gave me the names for all my kids (potential or actual). I will defend it to the death.

The latest you'd stay up to finish a book is...

A) I always fall asleep within about 10 pages.

B) If it's a really gripping thriller, I might see 2am.

C) Who needs sleep when you're desperate to know what happens?

MOSTLY As

Hey, have you ever even read a book (apart from this one)? It doesn't seem like it. So maybe you read a little here and there, but never try to compete with a true book lover, they'll take you down quicker than you can say "I only read celebrity autobiographies."

MOSTLY Bs

Sure, you like books. You've usually got one or two on the go and you can hold your own in a discussion about bestsellers. But... You do sometimes prefer an hour or two of Netflix.

MOSTLY Cs

OK, we know this is a book, so we're not exactly helping, but it might not be a bad idea to take a break from the books once in a while, buddy. You know, for a pee or a meal? What the hell are we saying, "CONGRATULATIONS BOOK NERD, WE ARE YOUR PEOPLE!"

The Bookseller

How did you get your hands on this book—maybe online or on someone's bathroom bookshelf (remember to wash your hands please)? Is it a semi-unwanted gift or did you actually walk into a store, interact with a human, and buy it in person? If it's the latter, you've just come across one of the most committed types of book lover, a person for whom the love of the written word is so great that they've dedicated their entire career to it (or they're in college and the job pays better than Starbucks, but let's gloss over that because it's not half as romantic). The Bookseller spends their whole life inhaling the rich scent of brand-new tomes, genre deciphering, novel recommending, running hands over luscious new front covers, and making the most of the staff discount. Sounds like heaven, right? Well let's remember that not every customer is such a delightful fellow book lover as your good self. Here are some of the shoppers booksellers love to hate:

The One Who Has Zero Details About the Book they Want

"I don't know what it's called, but it's by a man and it's got a river on the cover. I think I read it at school. There's a woman in it who might be called Mary. Do you know what it is?"

The One Who Wants You to Explain How an e-reader Works

The e-reader you didn't buy in store that you will use to download books, which are also not from their store. Seems like a fair exchange.

The Out-and-out Idiot

"Where can I find your fictional novels and your self-written autobiographies?"

The Cheapskate

"It costs how much? You know I could get this much cheaper if I buy it online, right?"

The Idiot, Part Two

"It's out of print? But can I order one for tomorrow though?"

The Misdirected Complainer

"I bought a book from here last week and I hated it, can I return it?" This is on a par with the guy who asks for coffee money back after an unsatisfactory date.

The Inconsiderate Gift Buyer

"I'm looking for a present for my girlfriend/mother/nephew that's got flowers/a woman/trucks on the cover, that'll do."

The Crèche Hunter

No, you cannot just leave your kids to run wild in the children's section while you browse erotica.

The Book Clubber

"But it's one of Oprah's, why don't you have it?" Because every other book sheep has already been in this morning to graze.

The Romantic vs The Sexophile

Heaving bosoms vs bruised buttocks. Euphemistically pleasant names for body parts vs graphic detail that'd make a gynecologist blush. All-encompassing kisses vs all-encompassing dungeon restraints. In a post-*Fifty Shades* world "romance" novels have taken on a whole new guise and for every dashing wartime soldier sweeping his sweetheart off her feet for a last embrace before he heads off to war there's a PVC-clad dominatrix stretching out her lover's scrotum on a customized rack. Unsure of which one you are? Here's how to tell...

How do you read your books?

A) On a Kindle. Always. Even when you're at home/in a bunker/ hiding in the cupboard under the stairs with your feet wedged against the door. And when out in public, following that incident where that gentleman of a certain age took reading page 73 over your shoulder as some kind of come on, you now always make sure the font is of a size that is illegible when viewed more than 4 inches away from the screen.

B) Dog-eared paperbacks. Once you get stuck in, they come everywhere with you.

A penis is?

A) Rarely in the singular.

B) A rising tumescence. Steel in velvet. Swelling in his loins.

You'd happily lend a copy to?

A) No one. Well, maybe Sarah at work. She's recently divorced and you've heard a rumor she's taken up an "experimental" lifestyle.

B) Your mother. In fact, did you borrow it from her?

The cover features?

A) Starkly shot implements of pain, perhaps a horsewhip, shadowed against silk, with a gold embossing that *American Pyscho* Patrick Bateman would kill for.

B) Breeches. Luscious flowing locks. A chest you could mistake for a cocker spaniel.

Your hero is called

A) Sir. Master. Daddy (eewww).
B) Lord Devalier-Smythe IV.

And your heroine is called?

A) Mistress. Pet. Good girl.
B) Miss Amelia Hornchurch.

Have you read *Fifty Shades*?

A) Of course. Even the last one. Well most of it anyway... Seriously, once the sex dried up did anyone get to the end?

B) You've left three book clubs for daring to suggest such a thing.

MOSTLY As

Congratulations, you're a fully fledged sexophile! Raised on a diet of Jackie Collins and Jilly Cooper, EL James filled a hole (pun very much intended) in your adult life for some good old-fashioned filth and set you back on the path of literotica. Just make sure your Kindle is password protected, hey.

MOSTLY Bs

Well done for picking up this book. We offer our sincerest apologies that there isn't a pair of cantilevered bosoms on the front cover, sitting atop a pair of rugged hands clasped powerfully around an impossibly tiny waist. You guessed it, you're a romantic, now get back to your story about that dashing Lord of the Manor and his below stairs (yep, another pun) activities, stat.

The Scholar

For most of us, once we leave school or complete our further education, reading is largely an activity carried out for pleasure. Sure there's the occasional tome on middle management you might have to pretend to read for work purposes, and you can't say you would describe all those pregnancy books as light entertainment. However, by and large you would agree that reading as an adult is an enjoyable, relaxed way to spend your free time.

This is definitely not the case for The Scholar, who attacks every piece of fiction as if he was about to compose a PhD thesis on the novel's subtextual use of weather, or the meaning of the mirror as analogy. If a scholar is in your book club, he will be the one that arrives with flashcards ready to present a 20-minute opening monologue, plus a printed list of "questions for discussion." (Incidentally, in this case "discussion" also means monologue— maybe the dictionary isn't a book he has got round to reading.)

Does this sound a little familiar? Try the quiz opposite to work out where you sit on the scholar spectrum.

You take notes in books when...

A) You don't have any other paper to hand and you need to note down a telephone number.

B) Are we talking just notes? Does that include underlining? Well, of course notes are made when you see a point you want to explore, research, or question. Everyone does that though, don't they?

If someone asks for your opinion of a book you've read do you...

A) Struggle for a couple of minutes to remember the story and then attempt to dredge up a few facts about the plot. Your summary will probably end with "Yeah, a good book to read on the beach."

B) Bring up a PowerPoint presentation on your iPhone and give them an introductory "chat" about key themes, before presenting them with a list of titles for further reading.

If someone disagrees with you about a book you...

A) Think there's a good chance you missed something when reading it.

B) Follow up with a 1,500-word email critiquing their points, complete with a bibliography for supporting evidence and citations written in the Harvard style.

At the book club your nickname is...

A) The White-wine Werewolf.

B) The English Professor.

How many of these words do you know the meaning of: abecedarium, anagnorisis, catachresis, deuteragonist, gnomic, polysyndenton?

A) Is that Welsh?

B) All of them.

MOSTLY As

You are a normal reader. You like to read books. In fact, you probably read one most days, but it's strictly a hobby.

MOSTLY Bs

You are dying to go back to school and become an English teacher. Why not do it? You're three-quarters of the way there already, you just need to finish sewing the elbow patches onto your tweed blazer.

The Non-finisher

This bookworm can be identified by the plaintive cry of "no spoilers please!" In every book discussion in your friendship group, just when you're getting going with your opinion, they'll pipe up with "Stop! I haven't got to that bit yet." When they say "yet," you know they mean "and never will," because for The N-F the final third of a novel is as unchartered territory as the icecaps of Greenland. What's behind The Non-finisher's refusal to reach the finish line?

The One Who Can't Commit

Looking for a significant other? Then be sure to take a glance at their bedside table before committing.* Are there more than three half-finished novels? Do weary spines give the impression these books have been sat face-down at the start of chapter 14 for a while? Do the novels vary wildly in their genres, from Scandi-noir to romance to fantasy? Looks like you've got yourself a commitment-phobe and if they can't even get to the end of a book then... Hang on a minute; is that Tinder they're swiping on their phone? You're still on your date?! Liberate the poor books from their neglect and get the hell out of there.

* Although, to be honest, if you've already got yourself in a position where you're eye level with their bedside table, then it might be too late for a sudden flee (unless you mention bowels—diarrhea will always save you).

The One Who Can't Concentrate

Scientists reckon in ten years we'll all have attention spans of approximately nine seconds,* so asking someone to sit down for around 14,400 seconds** is understandably nigh on impossible. Until technology invents a pair of glasses that can speed-read a book in the same amount of time it takes until you can skip the ads on a YouTube video, novels are lost on this sub-type.

* Well something like nine seconds anyway; we got bored halfway through reading the article and gave up.

** That's not the exact number of seconds it takes to complete the average novel, but we can't be bothered to work it out properly.

The One Who Likes Instant Gratification

Also known as the one who left Twitter in a fury (for a day anyway) when the 140-character limit was upped—"who has time, man?"—and all but lays down on the tracks in protest when a train is three, rather than two minutes away. If a story doesn't grab them in the first 20 pages, then it's got no chance.

The One Who is Just Too Damn Busy

"I wish I had time to read like you. I'd love to lounge around all day with a lovely novel, it's just with my multimillion-dollar business/13 children under five/part-time career as a UN ambassador AND my modeling commitments, I simply don't have the time."

The One Who Reads (Too Much?) Crime

When does a friend's forensic knowledge of, well, forensics become the kind of obsession that might warrant you making an anonymous tip-off to the police? Is it worrying that said friend knows exactly how to disguise the providence of a bullet or that the level of maggot infestation described in the autopsy denotes that a body has been dead a lot longer than police reports claim? Should you be more worried about your friend's bloodthirsty dive into the murky world of true crime than someone who can't get enough of Mafia and mobsters? Which crime fan are you?

The Gangster Aficionado

It started with a book on notorious East-End London gangsters the Kray twins, bought on a whim in an airport gift shop. You chose it because it was near the counter and was the only book you could see with a cover that wasn't embossed with gold italics and featuring a woman's legs in high heels walking through a generic cityscape. "This could be a decent enough read," you thought; and then, "OH MY GOD THIS IS MY WORLD! I want to dress like a pallbearer in an Italian wool suit. I like my mother. I've got a brother. OH JESUS IT COULD HAVE BEEN ME."

You find yourself dropping the odd bit of cockney rhyming slang into your everyday parlance. Brown bread* takes on a sinister meaning far from Warburtons and Wonder Bread, and you wouldn't Adam and Eve** what nonsense is coming out of that geezer's north and south.*** After devouring every Kray book you can buy on Amazon, you find yourself desperate enough to pick up anything that features a grainy black-and-white picture of a bald man and has an angry red typeface to display phrases like "on the run," "king of the streets," or "honor and death." Eventually, you close the London chapter of your gangster chronicles and move on to other organized crime groups—the Mafia, Chinese Triads, Japanese Yakuza, South American drug cartels, Scandinavian Hell's Angels, Jamaican Yardies— but nothing ever takes you back there to the high of that initial criminal discovery.

* Brown bread = dead; ** Adam and Eve = believe; *** North and south = mouth

The Historical Crime Reader

You consider yourself to be above other types of crime reader. You are unable to countenance those fools who are into Martina Cole, Karin Slaughter, and their ilk, reading about grubby little murders and lightly drawn detectives with issues. For you, it's all about the historical context when it comes to crime. You're actually learning something with your seven Jack the Ripper biographies and a shelf's worth of takes on the assassination of JFK.

The True Crime Fan

Much like people who harm animals are more likely to become serial killers, if you're deep into true crime then friends should be worried. FYI, if you start buying those magazines that say things like "I was murdered by my own false leg" or "the woman found with 17 severed scrotums in her freezer," then we're out.

The Dexter Obsessive

If you are captivated by Dexter the forensics scientist/serial killer, then chances are your friends have a WhatsApp group specifically devoted to "is <insert your name here> a bit creepy or what?" Sure, we all read Jeff Lindsay's first book about the blood-spatter expert who uses his skills to cover up his own crimes—and yep, we've watched one or two series of the TV version on Netflix—but we don't know the difference between the thickness of plastic sheets that will or will not allow for seepage that is detectable under a blue light. Because that'd be weird, right?

The Sci-fi Lover

Since nothing gets a sci-fi fan going more than some stats and facts, here's our list of the nine reasons you should love sci-fi too. So sweep aside those preconceptions about comedy spacesuits and shonkily put together monsters and open your mind.

1. It's Escapist

We have a lot of problems in our life and, you know, we don't always want to think about the global economy or consider the effects of climate change on the life cycles of wasps. Instead, we want to think about alternate universes, where they've never even heard of a thing called Trump.

2. It's For All Ages

From cuddly bug-eyed monsters who do good deeds to horrifying nuclear apocalypses, sci-fi is a genre that can grow with you.

3. It Predicts the Future

Instant messaging, Google glasses, iPads, 3D printers, facial scanning recognition, credit cards, FaceTime, sci-fi predicted the lot, so if you want to know what the world is going to look like in 50 years, we suggest you get reading.

4. ANYTHING Can Happen

You know those dull, workaday things that keep us tethered on earth—money, our bodies, gravity, public transport—NONE OF THESE EXIST! In the sci-fi universe you can fly to work or not go to work at all, because no one needs a job in the year 3010. We get a new body every six weeks, so we can eat, drink, and smoke whatever we want. But we don't even eat, drink, or smoke any more—we mind consume! Imagine any food and we are able to taste it, then... OK, you probably get the gist of this point.

5. It Teaches us Lessons

Don't wanna live in a terrifying dystopia? Let's look at how the characters got to that point. Not respecting the environment? Letting technology take over from human interaction? Hmmm, that sounds pretty familiar.

6. It Refreshes Your Mind

If you want to give your imagination a workout, then sci-fi is the brain equivalent of a 90-minute spin class. It's harder to imagine an entirely different world than it is another big city crime thriller or beachside bonkbuster, right?

7. It's Adventurous

Away from children's books, true adventure can be hard to find. We all know nostalgia is as hot as hell at the moment, so why not take a step back into the past by reading about the future?

8. It's a Safe Way to be Scared

We all like a spot of fear from time to time, it gets our adrenaline flowing. However, there's a huge difference between not being able to sleep for a week after reading about a predator who breaks into second-floor apartments in the middle of the night and murders brunette women in their late 20s, when you're a brunette woman in her 20s who, oh crap, lives in a second-floor apartment, and worrying about what happens when our family all become zombies.

9. It's Well Written

If you have never read anything by Isaac Asimov you're not qualified to argue with this.

The Fan

This particular bookworm would read the back of a cereal packet if his fave author wrote it. TBH, the RDA of niacin (WTF is niacin BTW?) would probably be a better read than the experimental poetry pamphlet The Fan's author crush wrote while at college, which was bought on eBay and cost an entire week's rent.

The fan lined up for four hours at a book signing and now owns a picture of him menacingly looming over his hero, holding the writer's shoulder almost as tightly as his bladder. He needed the toilet after an hour, but there was no way he was giving up his place. He definitely couldn't trust that awful woman stood behind him. She was obviously just going to sell her signed copy, she didn't even know the author had recently adopted a gerbil... And she had the cheek to call herself a fan.

That picture from the book signing is now in a frame, on his profile pic on every social media account he has (plus two new ones he opened just as an excuse to show it again), and is used as the screensavers for his phone and laptop. You suspect that come Christmas there might just be another sighting of the photo, only this time with the addition of crudely Photoshopped Santa hats.

When does fandom cross over to potential restraining order? Here are a few scenarios to watch out for:

1. Social Media

OK: Following your author on Twitter, Insta, Facebook, et al.
Kinda OK: Occasionally—OK, semi-regularly—replying to posts/retweeting/engaging in some fruitless way with your hero. They are a celebrated author with 4.2 million followers, you are but (admittedly quite persistent) man—they will never see your words.
Time to reign it in: Sending rambling 17-page letters plighting your troth for their work, written on paper that you've customized with tea/dirt/your own saliva to represent a key scene. Added stalker points if it's sent to the author's personal address that you bribed your cousin's boyfriend who is a policeman to look up for you.

2. Nomenclature

OK: Consider making one of your future child's middle names the same as an important character in your favorite book.

Kinda OK: Changing your name slightly in (what you think is) a comedy way on social media the day a new book is released.

Time to reign it in: Changing your name legally to your favorite character/bethrothed of the author themselves.

3. Personal Tributes

OK: Having a postcard of classic quotes from your favorite writer on your pin board, or a poster of a cool book cover on your wall.

Kinda OK: "Ironically" decorating your downstairs bathroom with a tribute to their work.

Time to reign it in: Getting a tattoo of their face, which covers your whole back and half of your left buttock.

4. Physical Attributes

OK: Dressing up as one of the characters for Halloween.

Kinda OK: Basing a dramatic new hairstyle/fashion overhaul on a character crush. That Lisbeth Salander undercut didn't go down so well at the call center, hey?

Time to reign it in: Breaking your own leg when your author suffers an accident so you "can feel closer to them."

The Faker

Of course, there's not a single chance of YOU being this person. You are a *bona fide* keen reader, you love books, you're reading one right now—surely that's proof enough, right? Fear not, there's no judgment here; we're sure you really did read every single novel, on every single shortlist, of every single major literary prize. Of course you did, but some people, unthinkable as it is, actually cheat when it comes to reading. Can you imagine?!

These people spout about the allegory, metaphors, themes, and subplots of all the latest literary big hitters, but you have a sneaking suspicion their reading actually consists of the two celebrity autobiographies they read on their annual summer vacations. Think you might have a faker on your hands? Here's how to bust one, plus a few tips on how to get away with a bit of faking yourself if you only "skimmed" the latest chart topper. Come on, even Graham Greene did it...

They Know Lots About the Author

That's the thing with googling information about a book instead of taking the time to actually read it. The first articles that come up will annoyingly tend to be interviews with the author talking about his or her life, inspiration, kids, and other such nonsense that won't help in an intense character motivation discussion with that book nerd Tom from accounts.

> Sample quote: *"I'm not sure you can really understand the 'coming of age as a teenager in a war zone' plot until you know about the writer's own challenging upbringing in the suburbs with two brothers and a mother who worked as a hairdresser."*

They Seem to Be a Little Forgetful

Sure they've got the lead character's name correct and they definitely know the first big twist, but anything that happens post the rough number of pages one can read in a train station while browsing in a bookstore is a little fuzzy.

Sample quote: *"Oh, it's easy to remember every detail about a book when you don't read much, but if you devour as many novels a week as I do then it's impossible to keep up."*

They Suddenly Go a Bit Existential

And question the whole subject of books and reading, shifting you as far from details as possible and onto "the wider context."

Sample quote: *"I think we really need to define what we mean by reading. Surely the point of stories is to be shared and does it matter if it's oral history or written?"*

They Use Non-arguable Opinions

A last-ditch attempt from a faker is to bring out that which can not really be argued about. Think off-limit dinner party topics and you're there. Ain't nobody who wants to find themselves on the wrong side of a sexism/racism/homophobic debate. Even if the book is solely about woodland animals.

Sample quote: *"I'm afraid I just found it very troubling from a misogyny angle. I just couldn't get on board with the underlying anti-female narrative."*

The (Not So) YA

There are certain teenage activities that if you, as a non-teenager, partook in you'd at best be considered a massive creep, at worst be in prison. So maybe put that idea of cheerleading try-outs and under-18 club nights away... BUT there's one teen activity that's totally fine (and no, it has nothing to do with sitting on your arm 'til it goes dead): indulging in some YA, (that's "young adult fiction" to those who are acronym averse or over 25 years old).

One of the fastest-growing genres in fiction, YA not only manages to defy the distractions of Snapchat, WhatsApp, and a million other technology-based things that we're too old to even know about, but it also snares a fair few readers for whom the Y can be skipped (or the A bookended with an O and a P). The grown-up YA reader can come in for some flack from YA refuseniks though, so it's useful to have a few retorts up your sleeve AND to know when you've gone too far...

HOW TO DEFEND YA

<u>They say:</u> The plots are basic.
<u>You say:</u> Actually, YA has to grip the reader from the start to deal with the decreasing teenage attention span. Therefore a good plot is needed that "hooks 'em in" within the first few pages.

<u>They say:</u> None of the characters have any depth.
<u>You say:</u> YOU HAVE CLEARLY NEVER HEARD OF KATNISS EVERDEEN!

They say: The writing is poor quality.
You say: It is good because it has to be. YA has neither the time or the page space for a 1,500-word description of the way the dust motes drift in a single shaft of light, so it picks the best description or dialog of the lot. Stripping text down to the bare bones means it has to work first time, every time.

They say: YA doesn't deal with serious issues.
You say: Love, loss, grief, mental health… None of these are big issues are they? Admittedly, most YA books don't deal with inequality in global education or the risk of volatile nuclear capability (FYI, some do— was anyone else permanently scarred by reading *Brother in the Land* at school?), but just 'cos the characters haven't reached their third decade it doesn't mean the plot's not serious.

They say: It's not relatable to adults.
You say: What even is an adult nowadays? Marriage, kids, owning a home… Yeah, that's really relatable for single millennials stuck in an 8-person house share until they're 42. TBH, that 16-year-old in your story who is wondering whether to text the guy back right away or leave it a bit has way more in common with the lives of a lot of 30-somethings than the whole nuclear family set up.

THINGS TO NEVER DO

Buy the merch: A backpack that's exactly the same as your fave hero's school bag. Nail varnish inspired by the color the heroine wore to prom. The ear cuff that you know you're 15 years too old for. It's cool to enjoy the books but leave all the merch to the teens.

Use the slang: This is just plain embarrassing. Adults have colonized the likes of OMG and LOL, but any deeper a dive into teen speak just makes you look like the kind of person whose IP address is on a list somewhere…

Try to talk to actual teens about it: Ever.

How to Upset
a Book Lover

Quite why you'd want to upset this largely inoffensive species is beyond us, but hey, no judgment here. So if a book lover in your life deserves a little kicking into touch here's what to say to get under their skin... And what to expect in retaliation.

ACTIONS TO GET REACTIONS

Action: "They're not real people you know."
Reaction: "How dare you silence me with a simple-but-effective takedown when I'm 10 minutes deep into a monologue about the motivation of the hero and how if only he'd taken a slightly different path then the whole ending would have been more realistic but not as emotive."

Action: "The movie version was considerably better."
Reaction: "THE MOVIE IS NEVER BETTER. The characters never look how I imagined them. The producers ALWAYS put in extra romance. The music will be all wrong. The director totally messed it up by relocating it. I'll give you *The Godfather* at a push, but that's it."

Action: "You've got too many books."
Reaction: "Actually I think you'll find I've got far too many friends. So I'd better start culling them. Beginning with you…"

Action: "What's your favorite book?"
Reaction: "How can I pick just one? Do you mean right now? Of all time? What about genre?" A descent into a spiral of panic follows.

Action: "Yeah, she dies at the end."
Reaction: "Don't we live in a world where spoilers are punishable by death yet? I'd vote for that policy."

Action: "I left that book you lent me on the bus."
Reaction: Cue a tantrum of full-on toddler meltdown proportions.

Action: "It's only a book."
Reaction: "And that was only your toe I just stamped on."

Action: "Is it on Netflix?"
Reaction: "No you imbecile, it's a book, you know the thing with pages that you probably haven't seen since school. Not this modern-day opiate for the masses you call Netflix."

Action: "Why don't you just write your own?"
Reaction: "Yeah because that makes sense. Why listen to music when you could sing to yourself? Why go to a restaurant when you could cook for yourself? Why watch a movie when you could act out all the parts in your living room? Why have sex when… OK, hopefully you get the message."

Action: "Ugh, Amy bought me books AGAIN for my birthday."
Reaction: "What? You mean Amy bought you the unequivocal pleasure of new reading material you ungrateful wretch."

Action: "Have you read all three *Fifty Shades...* books?"
Reaction: "Do I look like a twice-divorced soccer mom called Sandra?"

Action: "Don't you get bored reading all the time?"
Reaction: "Books can transport me to anywhere. Like somewhere that's not opposite an idiot like you."

The Technology Battle

If you want to cause a row between book lovers, there is no faster path to conflict than mentioning the K word... Yep, we said it, "Kindle." (Other e-readers are available but let's be honest, have you ever seen anyone using one?) Not known for being the most aggressive of species, a bibliophile tends to be of rather a placid nature most of the time. After all, books are scientifically proven to be calming you know. Well, the good ones are anyway. But now technology has reared its head and bookworms are forever divided. Here's a typical Kindle vs book altercation:

- **Kindle:** "Think of the trees, all that paper—it's just not eco-friendly."

- **Book:** "Actually, trees are both sustainable and renewable, unlike the potential toxic and non-breaking-down* materials used to make your e-reader."

- **Kindle:** "But it's so much cheaper to buy books this way."

- **Book:** "Don't you think an incredible book is worth a premium price? Who can put a price on pleasure?"

- **Kindle:** "Me, and it's around a third of the price you're paying. Plus, you can carry hundreds of books around with you."

- **Book:** "You only have one pair of eyes. What about the delicious smell of a new book?"

- **Kindle:** "Who smells books? You creep!"

- **Book:** "OK then, what about a beautiful front cover? Don't you want to be able to keep a physical object forever?"

- **Kindle:** "I've moved apartments 13 times in four years and I share a 100-square-foot space with two other people. Where the hell would I put a bookshelf?"

- **Book:** "You concentrate so much better on an actual book."

- **Kindle:** "What do you use at work? A quill?"

- **Book:** "You can loan your fave book to people."

- **Kindle:** "You treat yours like your firstborn. You've never lent me a book in our 15-year friendship."

- **Book:** "A book never breaks. You're on your third e-reader."

- **Kindle:** "Have you ever tried to read a book on a beach? Those pages go racing off faster than that waiter once he heard you were over 30."

- **Book:** "You're missing out on the experience of going into a bookstore."

- **Kindle:** "They're all coffee shops really now anyway. You have to fight your way through gluten-free lemon muffins and pumpkin spiced lattes to even get a whisper of a novel."

- **Book:** "The Internet connection on them never works."

- **Kindle:** "And where's the wi-fi hiding in a hardback?"

- **Book:** "The battery is always dying."

- **Kindle:** "The battery lasts longer than any of your boyfriends."

- **Book:** "I hate you."

* Yes, "non-breaking-down" is a recognized scientific term.**

** It's not a recognized scientific term.

15 Things All Bookworms Do

You can't consider yourself a true bookworm until you've done at least 10 of the following things...

1. Live in Denial About Shelf Space

You're sure you can squeeze in just. One. More. Book.

2. Tell Yourself: "Just One More Chapter..."

Even though it's 3am and you've got to get up in three hours.

3. Feel Personally Slighted When You Lend Someone Your Favorite Book and He or She Doesn't Like It

Can you even be friends any more? The jury's still out.

4. Judge People on the Train for Their Book Choices

Damn those commuters with their Kindles who are ruining this game.

5. Miss Your Stop on the Bus Because You've Been Too Engrossed in Your Book

Never mind, doubling back on yourself gives you more time to read.

6. Buy Multiple Versions of Your Favorite Books

"But this one has a different font on the cover! And the German version had limited-edition artwork!"

7. Feel More Invested in the Characters in Your Book Than Those Who Feature in Your Real Life

"NO ONE CARES about your kid's sports day, Janet from accounts," you scream to yourself, but you can name your heroine's shoe size and cereal preferences in a heartbeat.

8. Constantly Carry Around a Book

That micro bag trend is never going to work for you, because all your bags must be able to fit at least paperback. And tote bags must be branded with the name of your local bookstore or favorite publisher.

9. Pretend You'll Hold Out For the Paperback Because it's Cheaper...

Then cave in a day later because you can't wait several months to read it.

10. Grieve When a Book You Love Gets Made Into a Terrible Movie

It's doubly bad if they cast an actor you hate.

11. Let Books Guide Your Love Life

There's a definite connection there at the beginning, but you start to think twice about a potential boyfriend/girlfriend when they say that they don't like to read.

12. Have a Pinterest Board Devoted to Your Dream Library

One day that sanctuary lined with bookcases complete with a rolling ladder will be yours.

13. Cancel Plans to Stay In With Your New Book

All hail the NNS (which stands for new novel sickie), where social occasions are forsaken in favor of quality time with non-IRL friends.

14. Try to Read While Doing Other Things

Drying your hair/cooking/putting on makeup/a little minor surgery... It never ends well.

15. Donate Books to Charity Shops and Thrift Stores to Make Some Room in Your Home...

And then buy twice the number you gave away on the way out. "But they were SO cheap."

Index

Acknowledgments

For my mum and dad, who taught me to read by three (yep, I was a child prodigy) and started a lifelong love.

The publisher would like to thank Paul Parker for the illustrations, Eoghan O'Brien for the design, and Dawn Bates for proofreading.